D0208831

The National Portrait Gallery

The National Portrait Gallery was founded in
1856 to collect the likenesses of famous British
men and women. Today the collection is the most
comprehensive of its kind in the world, and
constitutes a unique record of the men and women
who created (and are still creating) the history and
culture of the nation. The Gallery houses a primary
collection of over nine thousand works, as well as an
immense archive. There is no restriction on medium
– there are oil paintings, watercolours, drawings,
miniatures, sculpture, caricatures, silhouettes and
photographs. The Gallery continues to develop its
role through its constantly changing displays, its
growing programme of international exhibitions, its
acquisitions and commissions, and the annual portrait
competition for young artists.

Introduction

A beautifully written inscription in Latin at the top of Gerlach Flicke's tiny self-portrait (p. 15) explains why he painted his portrait: '... This he himself painted from a looking-glass for his dear friends. That they might have something by which to remember him after his death.' The most obvious function of a portrait is commemorative: to record a person's appearance in a form that will outlive changes in the appearance, and, indeed, outlive the person. However, most portraits produced during Tudor times had more than a merely commemorative function. To assume that the Tudor artist's sole aim was to reproduce the sitter's features as accurately as possible for posterity is to overlook a complex set of factors affecting the production of portraits. Portraits were, on the whole, the product of an encounter between a number of different people with different interests and concerns: as well as the artist, there was a sitter, or sitters, there could have been a separate patron and there may have been another person still, the intended recipient. All these people could, and often did, influence both the artist's intentions and the appearance of the finished work. Trying to understand for what purposes and under what circumstances portraits were produced can help us to understand why portraits look the way they do. This is as true for Tudor portraits as it is for those produced today.

*fig. 1: Henry VI
by an unknown artist*

Leaving aside tomb sculpture, stained glass and manuscript illumination, there are very few surviving portraits of English sitters dating from before the beginning of the sixteenth century. A small amount of documentary material, the few portraits which do survive, and later copies of lost fifteenth-century paintings (figs. 1 and 2) indicate that portraits were produced in England before the Tudor period, but the evidence is so sparse that it is difficult to make general points about the nature of portraiture in England at this time. The earliest dated painting in the National Portrait Gallery is that of Henry VII, the founder of the Tudor dynasty (p. 8). This was produced as an aid to the marriage negotiations taking place between Henry and the widowed Margaret of Austria, Duchess of Savoy. The use of portraits in marriage negotiations, particularly between members of royal families, continued throughout the sixteenth century. Often the royal bride and groom met for the first time at the wedding ceremony, and the exchange of portraits beforehand was an essential part of the decision-making process. The recipient of such a portrait would necessarily be concerned that it should be as life-like as possible; however it might be to the advantage of the sender that the portrait should be flattering. This clash of interests sometimes resulted in rude shocks when the couple finally met. Philip II of Spain was said to have 'cursed the painters and envoys when he first beheld Queen Mary', for giving a misleading impression of her attractions (see p. 22).

Propaganda was another important function of royal portraiture. Hans Holbein's great mural of Henry VIII, his wife and parents (see p. 9) included a deliberately impressive and powerful image of the king. Although the mural seems to have been in a relatively private part of Whitehall Palace, it was the basis for numerous portraits of Henry that had wide circulation both in England and abroad. Viewers of these paintings would no doubt have been impressed by the magnificence and power of the image, and, by association, of Henry himself. The complex personal mythology which grew up around Elizabeth I, and which she used to maintain her sway over her people, was expressed in part through her portraits. Many of them compare her with biblical heroines and classical goddesses, and present her as eternally youthful, almost untouched by ordinary mortality. This apparent agelessness became increasingly important politically as the end of her life approached, with the succession in doubt, and the portraits painted of her in old age show her looking younger than ever. However, portraits of monarchs could be commissioned by people other than the monarch, and this led to the use of some images as negative propaganda. Elizabeth was aware of this,

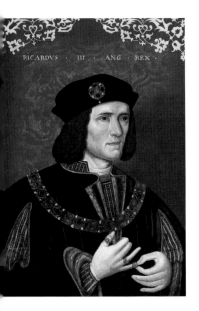

fig. 2: Richard III
by an unknown artist

and she made a number of attempts to control the production of her portraits. Orders were issued that unseemly portraits of her were to be destroyed, and a proclamation was drafted declaring that all her portraits should be versions of an approved image.

In addition to portraits of rulers, there was a great demand for images of other famous people of the day. Followers and relations of powerful men at court, such as Lord Burghley, owned portraits of them. The great interest in Mary, Queen of Scots after her captivity, particularly on the part of the French, led to the production not only of portraits of her, but of those associated with her, like her gaoler the Earl of Shrewsbury (see p. 29). Sir Francis Drake was so well-known during his lifetime that even in the Catholic countries where he was regarded as a heretic there was a demand for portraits of him, simply to satisfy people's curiosity as to his appearance. Some paintings of popular heroes, religious figures and villains were probably produced speculatively by artists, rather than to commission. They could be copied from well-known paintings or prints, or based on outlines transferred from studio patterns by various methods of tracing or pouncing (see pp. 9 and 11).

The demand for portraits of some sitters increased after their death. Those regarded as religious martyrs, such as Bishop John Fisher (see p. 11) and Sir

Thomas More (pp. 12-13) acquired a posthumous symbolic significance, and portraits were acquired by those in sympathy with their religious positions. One of the most interesting phenomena in posthumous portraiture during this period is the collection of sets of portraits of previous kings and queens of England. These were popular furnishings for the long galleries of country houses. In some cases the paintings appear to have been based on contemporary portraits, and so they can be regarded as reasonable likenesses (see p. 17, and also figs. 1 and 2, above). In other cases, where contemporary portraits were not available, the images were entirely invented.

Some of the most refined and sophisticated portraits produced during Tudor times are portrait miniatures; these seem to have often been commissioned as gifts for loved ones or followers of the sitter. They were sometimes kept in ivory or ebony boxes, or richly set in gold decorated with enamel and jewels. Whether worn on the clothing or held in the hand, their size meant that they were particularly intimate objects, and the richness of the setting added to their preciousness as a gift. The word 'miniature' actually refers to the watercolour medium used and the technique, which is like that of manuscript illumination, rather than to the size of the portrait; it derives from 'minium' which was a pigment used in manuscript illumination. For this reason, even larger scale works which would probably have been displayed on the wall can be called miniatures (see p. 36).

The Tudor portraits are among the most fascinating as well as the most mysterious works in the National Portrait Gallery. In the case of many, little is known about the circumstances in which they were produced; who, for example, was the recipient of Antonis Mor's portrait of Sir Henry Lee (p. 24), and why was Gerlach Flicke in prison (p. 15)? It may be that the answers to these questions are lost forever. However, far from diminishing their interest, this sense of mystery adds to the evocative qualities of particular images. Moreover, in addition to the clues which the portraits give us as to the lives and characters of those they depict, many testify to the tremendous abilities of the artists who created them, and so they can also be appreciated as some of the most outstanding artistic productions of an exceptional era.

HENRY VII
1457–1509
Unknown Netherlandish
artist, 1505
Oil on panel
42.5 x 30.5 cms

The founder of the Tudor dynasty, Henry VII was the son of Edmund Tudor, Earl of Richmond, and Margaret Beaufort. He became head of the House of Lancaster after the death of Henry VI, and in 1485 defeated Richard III at the Battle of Bosworth Field, the last of the Wars of the Roses. A year after he was crowned king he married Elizabeth of York, thus uniting the warring Houses of Lancaster and York. A notably clever king, he amassed enormous wealth for the Crown and established relative peace in England.

This is the earliest securely datable painting in the collection. The inscription on the frame records that it was painted on 29 October 1505 by the order of Herman Rinck, who was the agent of the Emperor Maximilian I. Rinck was involved in marriage negotiations between Henry VII and the widowed Margaret of Austria, Maximilian's daughter, and he brought two paintings of Margaret to England in 1505 for Henry. It seems that this portrait of Henry was produced by a Netherlandish artist for Margaret. Nothing came of the negotiations in the end, but the portrait apparently hung in her palace in Mechelen until her death in 1530.

HENRY VII AND HENRY VIII

Hans Holbein, *c.1536–1537*
Ink and water-colour on
paper mounted on canvas
257.8 x 137.2 cms

This majestic image of Henry VIII (1491–1547), with his father Henry VII (1457–1509) in the background, is part of a preparatory drawing for a great wall painting in Whitehall Palace. The completed mural showed the two kings on the left, with their queens, Elizabeth of York and Jane Seymour, on the right, and in between a stone tablet inscribed with verses celebrating the Tudor dynasty. The inscription also included the date, 1537, which was the year Henry VIII's son by Jane Seymour, Edward, was born. The mural was destroyed when the palace burned down in 1698, but a seventeenth-century copy records its full appearance.

This drawing, or 'cartoon', which is the actual size of the mural, consists of a number of sheets of paper joined together. The heads of the kings have been cut out from separate sheets and pasted on to backing paper. The cartoon was used to transfer the composition to the wall by a method called pouncing. All the important outlines of the drawing were pierced with tiny holes, still visible, and the paper was then attached to the wall where the painting was to be. Charcoal dust was brushed into the holes, leaving lines of tiny black dots marking the outlines on the wall. When the paper was removed, Holbein could start painting, using the charcoal as guidelines.

(Enlarged)

THOMAS CROMWELL,
1ST EARL OF ESSEX
1485–1540
Hans Holbein, *c.*1532–1533
Miniature on vellum
4.4 cms (diameter)

From a relatively obscure background, Cromwell worked his way up the social and political ladder to become one of the most powerful men in England. He implemented the reforms that established Henry VIII as the head of the Church in England, and ruthlessly oversaw the dissolution of the monasteries. He also negotiated Henry's fourth marriage, to Anne of Cleves, and was created Earl of Essex, but he lost favour when the marriage failed. Accused of treason by the Duke of Norfolk, the king did not intervene on his behalf, and he was executed in 1540.

Holbein, whose home was in Basel, worked in a variety of different media on a wide range of scales, from magnificent wall paintings (see previous page), to sensitive chalk drawings, and exquisite miniatures like this one. The works produced by him during his two visits to England, from 1526 to 1528, and from 1532 until his death in 1543, include some of the most extraordinary portraits ever produced in this country. Cromwell was one of Holbein's most important patrons during the artist's second visit, although this is the only surviving portrait of Cromwell which is generally agreed to be by the artist.

JOHN FISHER,
BISHOP OF
ROCHESTER
1459–1535
Unknown artist
Oil on paper
21 x 19.1 cms

Martyred for his opposition to Henry VIII's divorce from Catherine of Aragon and his refusal to accept the king as the head of the Church in England, Fisher had been a Professor of Divinity and Chancellor of Cambridge University, and Bishop of Rochester. In 1935 he was canonised as a saint.

This sympathetic portrait was copied from another drawing, now lost, by a method of transfer called pouncing (see p. 9). Tiny black dots are visible along the main outlines of Fisher's head, shoulders and hat. In the past these were thought to be holes to enable the composition to be transferred on to another surface. However, recent conservation and microscopic examination has shown that the black dots are not holes but tiny mounds, probably of charcoal, on the surface of the paper, showing that this drawing was the result, not the means of a transfer process. The drawing was probably kept in an artist's workshop as a pattern on which to base other repetitions of Fisher's portrait, but no contemporary completed versions of the portrait are known today. The prime version of this image is a drawing by Hans Holbein, in the Royal Collection.

SIR THOMAS MORE, HIS FATHER,
HIS HOUSEHOLD AND HIS DESCENDANTS
Rowland Lockey, 1593
Oil on canvas
227.4 x 330.2 cms

In the winter of 1526 Holbein arrived in England with a letter of introduction from Erasmus to Sir Thomas More (1478–1535), the famous humanist and later Lord Chancellor of England. In the following year he began a great painting of More and his family, a celebration of dynasty, family piety and learning. Holbein's painting was almost certainly destroyed during the eighteenth century, but its appearance is recorded in a copy and a preliminary drawing.

This painting is an adaptation of his group portrait, probably commissioned by More's grandson, Thomas More II, to commemorate five generations of the family. The four figures wearing ruffs and holding prayerbooks on the right-hand side are Thomas More II, his wife and their oldest and youngest sons. The other seven figures, copied from Holbein's original family group, are Sir Thomas More with his father, his three daughters, his son and his son's wife, who also appears as an older woman in the portrait hanging on the wall. The demand for copies and versions of Holbein's portrait was no doubt fuelled by the perception of Sir Thomas More as a Catholic martyr; he had been executed by Henry VIII in 1535 after refusing to accept the king as head of the English Church. The later generations of the More family are presented here as continuing not only the family line but also the family faith, represented by their prayerbooks and crucifixes.

ARCHBISHOP
THOMAS CRANMER
1489–1556
Gerlach Flicke, 1545
Oil on panel
98.4 x 76.2 cms

Cranmer was Archbishop of Canterbury from 1533, and the architect of Henry VIII's divorce from Catherine of Aragon. Throughout his public career he struggled to reconcile his theological views with his loyalty to the king, at times at the expense of his integrity. Unlike many of his contemporaries he managed to stay in favour with Henry throughout his reign, but he was burned at the stake for heresy by Mary I.

This is the earliest known work by Gerlach Flicke, a German artist working in London during the 1540s and 1550s. His name is inscribed at the top of the stone casement. Below this, on a piece of paper or vellum attached to the casement with red wax, is written in Latin, 'In his 57th year July 20'; this refers to Cranmer. Flicke has portrayed the Archbishop as a Protestant reformer, surrounded by books, reflecting his concerns for the authority of the Word of God.

GERLACH FLICKE AND HENRY STRANGWISH
Gerlach Flicke, 1554
Oil on paper or vellum on panel
8.8 x 11.9 cms

The beautifully written inscriptions at the top of this tiny double portrait identify the sitters. Above Flicke (fl. 1545–1558), shown holding a palette, the inscription is in Latin and can be translated: 'Such was the face of Gerlach Flicke when he was a painter in the City of London. This he himself painted from a looking-glass for his dear friends. That they might have something by which to remember him after his death.' On the right, above Henry Strangwish, the inscription reads: 'Strangwish, thus strangely depicted is One prisoner, for thother, hath done this/Gerlin, hath garnisht, for his delight This woorck whiche you se, before youre sight.'

As this implies, the portrait was painted when the two men were in prison, probably the Tower of London. Henry Strangwish was a gentleman pirate from the West Country. He was later reprieved by Elizabeth I, and, along with other pirates of good family, entered the Queen's service. Little is known about Flicke other than that he came from Osnabrück in Germany and was working in England by 1545. It is not known why he was incarcerated. His portrait is the earliest known oil self-portrait produced in England.

CATHERINE OF
ARAGON
1485–1536
Unknown artist, *c.*1530
Oil on panel
55.9 x 44.5 cms

Married first to Prince Arthur, the elder brother of Henry VIII, Catherine was the youngest child of Ferdinand and Isabella of Spain, and so an important political pawn. Arthur died in 1502, and it was agreed that Catherine should marry Henry, which she did shortly after his coronation. Apparently happy together at first, Catherine's only surviving child was a girl, Princess Mary (later Mary I), which was a great disappointment. Eager for a son and keen to marry his mistress, Anne Boleyn, Henry began to investigate the possibilities of a divorce. Eventually the marriage was annulled by Archbishop Cranmer in 1533, after years of debate and humiliation for Catherine. It was a momentous step, leading to Henry's excommunication by the Pope and the severing of the connection between the Church in England and the Church in Rome.

Catherine's behaviour throughout her long ordeal was consistently dignified. An Italian visitor to London in 1531 described her as 'prudent and good ... During these differences with the King she has evinced constancy and resolution, never being disheartened or depressed'. He went on to say that she was 'not of tall stature, rather small. If not handsome she is not ugly; she is somewhat stout and has always a smile on her countenance.'

ANNE BOLEYN
1507–1536
Unknown artist
Oil on panel
54.3 x 41.6 cms

Henry VIII married his second wife, Anne Boleyn, in secret in January 1533, shortly before his marriage to Catherine of Aragon was annulled. Their daughter, Princess Elizabeth, was born in September of the same year. Anne was the daughter of Sir Thomas Boleyn, and a cousin of Henry's fifth and equally doomed wife Catherine Howard. Unfortunately she did not produce the longed-for male heir, and Henry, tiring of her, had her charged with adultery with several people, including her own brother, and beheaded.

Anne was described by a contemporary as 'not one of the handsomest women in the world; she is of middling stature, swarthy complexion, long neck, wide mouth, bosom not much raised, and in fact has nothing but the English King's great appetite, and her eyes, which are black and beautiful'. This is a good example of the type of portrait of Anne included in the sets of kings and queens which were produced for long galleries during the sixteenth and early seventeenth centuries. Anne's identity is reinforced by the 'B' jewel around her neck.

CATHERINE PARR
1512–1548
Master John, *c.*1545
Oil on panel
180.3 x 94 cms

The sixth and last wife of Henry VIII, Catherine was about to marry Thomas Seymour, Lord Sudeley, when she caught the attention of the king and was forced to marry him instead. She showed great kindness to his children by previous marriages, persuading Henry to reinstate Mary and Elizabeth in the succession, bringing them into her household and supervising their and Edward's education. She was a faithful companion to the king in his last years, nursing his ulcerated leg and on occasions discussing theology with him. Shortly after Henry's death Catherine at last married Thomas Seymour, but her happiness was short-lived: she died in childbirth a year later.

Previously thought to be Lady Jane Grey, the sitter in this portrait has recently been re-identified as Catherine Parr. She is shown in a pose used by Holbein for his portraits of potential royal brides. She is wearing a splendid dress of cloth of silver lined with lynx fur, over a crimson underskirt embroidered with gold and pearls. The distinctive crown-headed brooch pinned to her dress has been identified in Catherine Parr's jewellery inventories. Little is known of 'Master John', whose portrait of Princess Mary from 1544 is also in the collection.

EDWARD VI
1537–1553
Unknown artist
Oil on panel
155.6 x 81.3 cms

The precocious son of Henry VIII
and his third wife, Jane Seymour,
Edward came to the throne at the
age of nine, early in 1537. His
reign was marked by the influence
of his two protectors, first the Duke of Somerset and then the Duke of
Northumberland, and by the radical reformation of the Church, which included
the widespread destruction of holy images. Edward VI died of tuberculosis shortly
before his sixteenth birthday.

This portrait probably dates from about the time Edward became king, although it
is based on an earlier painting. The stance of the young king deliberately echoes
that of his father Henry VIII in Holbein's Whitehall mural (see p. 9), reinforcing
Edward's Tudor heritage and conveying the sense of the authority Henry has in
the earlier portrait. This is a particularly richly made portrait; gold leaf is used
extensively, and the red of Edward's cloak is painted over a layer of silver leaf.

EDWARD VI
1537–1553
Gwillim Scrots, 1546
Oil on panel
42.5 x 160 cms

Known as an anamorphosis, this extraordinary portrait is primarily a display of technical virtuosity on the part of the painter. When viewed through a hole on the right-hand side of the frame, the perspective corrects itself and a conventional profile portrait of Edward VI aged 9 becomes apparent. Other painted and engraved portraits using this kind of perspectival distortion were produced in the court of the Habsburg Emperor Charles V during the middle of the sixteenth century. Gwillim Scrots had been employed by the Emperor's sister, Mary of Hungary; he came to work in England for Henry VIII in 1545. In the eighteenth century an inscription, 'Guihelmus pingebat' (William painted this), was visible on the frame.

MARY I
1516–1558
Hans Eworth, 1554
Oil on panel
21.6 x 16.9 cms

The only surviving child of Henry VIII and Catherine of Aragon, Mary came to the throne after the brief 'reign' of Lady Jane Grey, as the first queen regnant of England. A fervent Roman Catholic, she reconciled England with the Papacy, and was popular at the beginning of her reign. However, her marriage to Philip II of Spain, persecution of English Protestants, and the war with France, ensured that she was deeply unpopular by the time of her death. Suffering from ill-health throughout adulthood, she falsely believed herself to be pregnant on more than one occasion. Her marriage was not successful, and it was claimed that her unhappiness at Philip's absence contributed to her final illness.

Hans Eworth was the most significant artist working in England in the generation after Holbein. Originally from the Netherlands, he made his career in London for almost thirty years. Mary I was his most important patron and he produced a number of variants of this portrait. It may be that this is a flattering likeness: Mary was considered pretty as a young woman, but by 1554 her age was thought to be against her. Philip is said to have cursed her painters when he first met her, for having exaggerated her attractions.

ELIZABETH I
1533–1603
Marcus Gheerhaerts
the Younger, *c.*1592
Oil on canvas
241.3 x 152.4 cms

The legendary 'Virgin Queen', Elizabeth I was the daughter of Henry VIII and his second, ill-fated wife, Anne Boleyn. Elizabeth had maintained her Protestant beliefs during the reign of her half-sister Mary, and on her accession determined to restore England to Protestantism. Her own strength of character and the ability of her ministers ensured that the age was on the whole one of peace and prosperity. The might of her sea captains and the development of exploration and trade enabled England under Elizabeth to become a world power.

Known as the 'Ditchley Portrait', this painting was probably commissioned by Sir Henry Lee (see next page), to commemorate an elaborate symbolic entertainment he organised for Elizabeth in September 1592. After retiring from his role as Queen's Champion in 1590, Lee lived at Ditchley in Oxfordshire with this mistress Anne Vavasour, much to the queen's anger. The entertainment, held either at Ditchley or at the nearby palace of Woodstock, marked the queen's forgiveness of her favourite for becoming 'a stranger lady's thrall'. She is shown standing on the globe of the world, with her feet approximately on Oxfordshire. The stormy sky, the clouds parting to reveal sunshine, and the inscriptions on the painting make it plain that the portrait's symbolic theme is forgiveness.

SIR HENRY LEE
1533–1611
Antonis Mor, 1568
Oil on panel
64.1 x 53.3 cms

Elizabeth's Master of the Ordnance and one of her favourites, Henry Lee was the originator of the Accession Day Tilts, the most important Elizabethan court festivals from at least 1581. These were elaborate spectacles combining jousting, poetry, music and theatre.

Lee had his portrait painted on a visit to Antwerp, where Antonis Mor, one of the most accomplished portrait painters in Europe during the sixteenth century, was working at the time. The true-lovers' knots on Lee's sleeves, the prominence of the rings and the use of red suggest that Lee is presented here as a lover, possibly as a courtly lover of the queen herself: armillary spheres like those on Lee's sleeves are associated with Elizabeth I, and black and white were her personal colours. On the other hand, it would seem likely that if she were the beloved object, she might have been given the painting, but it came to the Gallery from Lee's own descendants. It may be that it was instead a gift to his wife or mistress.

LADY MARY NEVILLE AND HER SON
GREGORY FIENNES, 10TH BARON DACRE
Hans Eworth, 1559
Oil on panel
50 x 71.4 cms

This beautifully executed double portrait is generally regarded as Eworth's master-piece in the art of portraiture. It was apparently painted to mark the restoration of honour and titles to the family of Thomas, 9th Baron Dacre in 1559. Lord Dacre had been executed during the reign of Henry VIII for his part in a poaching expedition during which a gamekeeper was killed. His title and honours were forfeited, and his family disgraced. His widow, Mary Neville (1524–1576) re-married twice but continued to be concerned about her first husband's honours, particularly in so far as they affected her children. She is depicted here with her eldest son, the newly created 10th Baron. It is extremely unusual for a portrait of this period to show a mother and son together, rather than a husband and wife, and it perhaps reflects the dominance of this particular mother. Gregory's wife, Anne Sackville, apparently complained that he remained under the influence of his mother after his marriage, and Gregory himself is said to have been 'a little Crack-brain'd'.

WILLIAM CECIL,
1ST BARON
BURGHLEY
1520–1598
By or after Arnold van
Brounckhorst,
c.1560–1570
Oil on panel
95. 3 x 71.8 cms

Elizabeth's first appointment when she ascended the throne was to make William Cecil her principal secretary of state; he became the youngest member of her council. Throughout his life he was the queen's most influential minister, tempering her actions with cautious but decisive advice. He was created Baron Burghley in 1571, and Lord High Treasurer and chief minister in 1572. He only once fell from favour, over the execution of Mary, Queen of Scots. Elizabeth had signed the death warrant, but she later claimed that she had never intended the execution to take place, and blamed Burghley, who had long advocated it.

The only real threat to Burghley's influence over the queen came from the Earl of Leicester. 'A light and greedy man', Leicester was Elizabeth's one serious English suitor, and her favourite from the beginning of her reign until his death. Appointed Master of the Horse at her accession, he was made a Knight of the Garter and Privy Councillor the following year. His attempts to marry the queen were thwarted by Burghley, who tried to curb his power and influence. Leicester

ROBERT DUDLEY,
EARL OF LEICESTER
1532–1588
Unknown artist, *c.*1575
Oil on panel
108 x 82.6 cms

commanded the unsuccessful force against Spain in the Netherlands, and was involved in a number of scandals and intrigues.

As well as their dislike of one another, Burghley and Leicester shared an exceptional interest in their own portraiture. The differences in their surviving portraits illustrate well the differences in their characters. More contemporary portraits of Burghley exist than of any Elizabethan other than the queen herself. However, they derive from only three main types: Burghley's patronage was directed specifically towards the production and reproduction of a carefully controlled image of himself, for the purposes of propaganda. By contrast, more types of portraits of Leicester exist than of any other courtier, testifying to his great love of finery and his personal vanity.

MARY, QUEEN
OF SCOTS, 1542–1587
Unknown artist, *c.*1610
Oil on panel
79.1 x 90.2 cms

The daughter of Mary of Guise and James V of Scotland, Mary Stuart succeeded to the throne of Scotland as an infant. She was brought up a Roman Catholic and spent most of her childhood in France, where she married the French king Francis II in 1558. From the death of Mary I, she laid claim to the English throne, as a great-granddaughter of Henry VII. After her husband's death she returned to Scotland, where she reigned for seven turbulent years, in which she married Lord Darnley, witnessed the murder of her favourite, Riccio, connived with the Earl of Bothwell at Darnley's murder, and then married Bothwell. Finally she was forced to flee to England, where she was held captive for twenty years. As a focus for Roman Catholic rebellion, Mary represented a continual threat to Elizabeth I, who finally agreed to her execution in 1587.

This is a good example of the most popular type of portrait of the queen. Many versions exist, most thought to be posthumous, and probably all deriving from a miniature by Nicholas Hilliard. The inscription records that she is shown during the thirty-sixth year of her age and reign, and the tenth year of her captivity by the English. The description of Mary as 'most pious' in the inscription, the prominence of the rosary and crucifix, and the scene of Susannah and the Elders in the centre of the crucifix (symbolising the triumph of right through divine aid) all imply that the painting was produced for a Catholic family.

GEORGE TALBOT, 6TH EARL OF SHREWSBURY
*c.*1522–1590
Unknown artist, *c.*1580
Black, brown and red chalk on paper
33 x 22.5 cms

One of Elizabeth's most trusted courtiers, Shrewsbury was rewarded for his faith-fulness by being made gaoler of Mary, Queen of Scots for sixteen years. Fourteen of those years were spent at Sheffield Castle, during which time the Earl requested on several occasions that he be relieved of his onerous responsibilities. Additional difficulties were created by the increasing enmity between Shrewsbury and his second wife, 'Bess of Hardwick', which culminated in 1583 in Bess circulating rumours that an 'improper intimacy' existed between her husband and the Queen of Scots.

This portrait of Shrewsbury is the earliest chalk drawing in the collection. It appears to be the work of a French artist, and the inscription at the top, in French, records that it was produced at Sheffield Castle. There was a continuing French interest in the captive Scottish queen and her circumstances, and the drawing was probably made for one of Mary's supporters in France. The inscription appears to be a later addition, and the date may not be correct, as other versions of this portrait date from 1580.

(Enlarged)

SIR FRANCIS DRAKE
1540–1596
Nicholas Hilliard, 1581
Miniature on vellum
2.8 cms (diameter)

The greatest hero of English seafaring, recognised in his lifetime as well as by posterity, Drake was an outstandingly successful navigator, and also a privateer. During his circumnavigation of the globe from 1577–1580 he amassed a fortune for both the Treasury and for himself through piracy. Subsequently Elizabeth I and her ministers encouraged his activities, intending that his attacks on Spanish ships should weaken the Spanish navy as well as diverting the proceeds of trade into English coffers. Drake was vice-admiral of the fleet sent against the Spanish Armada in 1588, and although his role in the victory was not the decisive one, it is his name that continues to be associated with the battle.

Although relatively few images of Drake survive, there is evidence that numerous portraits were produced during his lifetime, both in England and on the continent. This miniature was painted in the year he was knighted; his appearance corresponds well with the description of a contemporary: ' ... round headed, browne hayre, full Bearded, his eyes round, large and cleare, well favoured, fayre, and of a cheerefull countenance'.

SIR WALTER RALEGH
1552–1618
Nicholas Hilliard, *c.*1585
Miniature on vellum
4.8 x 3.9 cms   *(Enlarged)*

The consummate 'renaissance man', Ralegh was an accomplished poet and writer as well as an explorer. Much of his poetry is lost, but his surviving works include about thirty short pieces and a narrative, *The History of the World*. He attempted to establish colonies in America and is credited with introducing tobacco and potatoes to England. He played a brilliant part in the expeditions to Cadiz and the Azores, and made several attempts to find gold in South America. Like most of her favourites, Ralegh was alternately in and out of favour with Elizabeth I. He conspired with Spain against James I and was executed for treason.

Nicholas Hilliard's extraordinarily meticulous technique and refined, relatively flat and decorative style helped him to become one of the most famous artists of Elizabethan England. He produced numerous exquisite miniature portraits of the queen and of members of her court, precious and particularly intimate portraits which were sometimes encased in elaborate enamelled or jewelled settings and worn on the clothing.

This extraordinary painting is a memorial to Sir Henry Unton, an Elizabethan soldier and diplomat who died in France. On the right-hand side scenes of the important events in Unton's life surround a group of domestic scenes set in his house. In the middle of the painting is Unton's portrait, with allegorical figures representing Death and Fame on either side of his head. At the left is his funeral, the procession issuing from the doors of his house on the right and stretching across the painting.

The scenes are as follows (moving anti-clockwise from the bottom right-hand corner):

- As a baby in the arms of his mother, Anne Seymour, formerly Countess of Warwick, *c*.1557
- Studying at Oriel College, Oxford, *c*.1573
- Travelling to Venice and Padua, 1570s. (The Alps are in the background.)
- Serving as a soldier with the Earl of Leicester in the Netherlands, where he was knighted after the battle of Zutphen in 1586

SIR HENRY UNTON
1557?–1596
Unknown artist, 1596
Oil on panel
74 x 163.2 cms

- Riding towards the town of Coucy La Fère as ambassador to Henry IV, 1595–6
- Sick with a fever; a physician visiting him, February 1596
- A ship with black sails crossing the Channel, bringing his body home to England
- His hearse travelling along the road towards the Unton family home, Wadley House, at Faringdon near Oxford
- (centre right) Unton's home life, with scenes of him in his study (top), making music (top left), talking with learned divines (bottom left), and presiding over a banquet, entertained by a masque of Mercury and Diana with a musical accompaniment
- The funeral procession, leading from the doors of the house, passes a group of poor people bemoaning Unton's death, and enters the church where the funeral is taking place. In front of the church is Unton's monument, with his widow, who commissioned this painting, kneeling behind the recumbent effigy.

SIR PHILIP SIDNEY
1544–1586
Unknown artist, *c*.1576
Oil on panel
113.9 x 84 cms

A brave soldier, effective diplomat and gifted writer in prose and poetry, to his contemporaries Sidney represented the ideal of the renaissance courtier. He was one of the most influential of all Elizabethan poets, known particularly for his prose romance *Arcadia* and the sonnet sequence *Astrophel and Stella*. He died of wounds received fighting the Spanish at the Battle of Zutphen, and was deeply mourned: two hundred poetic memorials were written in his honour.

Sidney had had smallpox as a child, which according to a contemporary had 'laid waste, as with little mines, the excellence and fashion of his beauty'. Ben Jonson, who probably had not seen him, described him as 'no pleasant man in countenance, his face being spoiled with pimples & of high blood & long'. In this painting, however, the perfection of his character seems to have affected the depiction of his appearance. The Latin motto, probably added posthumously, can be translated as 'the rest is fame'.

MARY SIDNEY,
COUNTESS OF
PEMBROKE
1561–1621
Nicholas Hilliard, *c*.1590
Miniature on vellum
5.4 cms (diameter)   *(Enlarged)*

A writer and patron of writers, it was at Mary Sidney's suggestion that her brother Philip (see opposite page) wrote his celebrated *Arcadia*. She worked together with Sidney on a metrical translation of the Psalms, and after his death took under her protection many of the writers to whom he had acted as patron. Like many able women of this period in England, her achievements have traditionally been measured in terms of her relationships with important men: her epitaph records her as 'Sidney's sister, Pembroke's mother'.

This miniature is one of a group produced by Hilliard depicting members of the circle of Robert Dudley, Earl of Leicester (see p. 27) who was Hilliard's great patron. The strings of pearls around the countess's neck have been executed in Hilliard's characteristic manner, with burnished silver highlights; the silver has oxidised, and has turned them black.

ROBERT DEVEREUX,
2ND EARL OF ESSEX
1566–1601
Attributed to Nicholas
Hilliard, *c.*1587
Miniature on vellum
24.8 x 20.3 cms

Elizabeth's last favourite, 'a nature not to be ruled', Essex was the hot-headed and ambitious stepson of the Earl of Leicester. In his early years at court the queen was captivated by him and he was with her constantly, so that 'he cometh not to his own lodging till birds sing in the morning'. He wrote poetry, was a patron of writers and took a leading role in the annual Accession Day Tilts. Confirmed as a popular hero when he took Cadiz, he subsequently lost his place at court as a result of his high-handed behaviour as governor-general of Ireland. With an inflated idea of his own power and importance, he tried to raise a rebellion against the queen's ministers in 1601. The rebellion failed and Essex was executed for treason.

Essex is depicted here in elaborate armour, on which is embroidered his *impresa*, diamonds within a circle, with the motto 'Dum formas minuis'. The miniature dates from the period of Essex's early favour with the queen, and shows him before he grew a beard. He may be dressed for jousting at a court festival, or the setting may be intended to be one of the battles in the Netherlands in which he played an important part. The authorship of this miniature has been the matter of much scholarly debate; it may well be by an as yet unidentified artist.

(Enlarged)

ISAAC OLIVER
*c.*1565–1617
Self-portrait, *c.*1590
Miniature on vellum
6.2 x 5 cms

A Huguenot refugee from France, Isaac Oliver came to England with his family when he was a child. He seems to have worked with Nicholas Hilliard at some point, perhaps only briefly, but the style of his miniature painting is particularly distinguished from Hilliard's by softer modelling and the much greater use of shadows. Oliver was apparently not favoured by Queen Elizabeth I, but after her death he was appointed miniaturist to Anne of Denmark, and later to Henry, Prince of Wales, James I's elder son.

This magnificent miniature is one of two self-portraits by Oliver. It once belonged to Horace Walpole, who said of it, 'The art of the master and the imitation of nature are so great in it that the largest magnifying-glass only calls out new beauties.'

WILLIAM
SHAKESPEARE
1564–1616
Attributed to John Taylor
(d. 1651)
Oil on canvas
55.2 x 43.8 cms

The most celebrated English playwright and poet, Shakespeare is generally considered to be one of the greatest writers of all time. The extraordinary admiration with which he is regarded has created a tremendous fascination with his appearance, and thus a huge demand, posthumously, for portraits of him. Over the centuries many portraits have been thought to represent him. In fact, apart from his tomb monument and the engraving that accompanied the early folio editions of his plays, only this painting can reasonably be regarded as a true depiction.

Very little is known about John Taylor. The painting is known as 'the Chandos portrait' after one of its eighteenth century owners, the Duke of Chandos. It was the very first painting to enter the National Portrait Gallery collections, in 1856.

All illustrations are copyright the National Portrait
Gallery, except p. 25, © reserved

Published by National Portrait Gallery Publications
National Portrait Gallery
St Martin's Place
London   WC2H 0HE

Copyright © National Portrait Gallery, 1996

All rights reserved. No part of this publication may be
reproduced, stored in a retrieval system or transmitted in
any form or by any means, electronic, mechanical, including
photocopying, recording or otherwise, without the prior
written consent of the publisher

ISBN 1–85514–207–4

Written by Catharine MacLeod
Designed by Mark Reynolds
Printed by Amica Fine Art Print Ltd

NPG